20th Century Lives

MEDICAL PIONEERS

Debbie Foy

WAYLAND

First published in 2009 by Wayland

Copyright © Wayland 2009

Wayland
338 Euston Road
London NW1 3BH

Wayland
Hachette Children's Books
Level 17/207 Kent Street
Sydney, NSW 2000

Designer: Jason Billin
Editor: Nicola Edwards

British Library Cataloguing in Publication Data
Foy, Debbie.
Medical pioneers. -- (20th century lives)
1. Medical innovations--History--20th century--Juvenile literature.
2. Medical scientists--Biography--Juvenile literature.
3. Physicians--Biography--Juvenile literature.
I. Title II. Series
610.9'22-dc22

ISBN: 978-0-7502-5823-4

Printed in China

Wayland is a division of Hachette Children's Books, an Hachette UK Company.

Picture acknowledgements:

Cover: Getty Images:Keystone; title page: Rex Features: Everett Collection
Camera Press, London: Keystone-France/Eyedea p19; Corbis: Bettmann p13, Ted Spiegel p14,
Bettmann p17; Getty Images: Harold Clements/Daily Express/Hulton Archive p4, Frederic
J.Brown/AFP p5, Alfred Eisenstaedt/Pix Inc/Time & Life Pictures p6, Hulton Archive p11,
Keystone p18, Keystone p24, Hulton Archive p26, Fritz Goro/Time Life Pictures p28, Sven
Nackstrand/AFP p29; London Borough of Lambeth, Lambeth Archives Department: p2, p23;
PA Photos: Barratts p8, AP Photo/Gurinder Osan p20, AP Photo/Gurinder Osan p21; Rex
Features: Everett Collection p1, Everett Collection p12; Science Photo Library: A.Barrington
Brown p15, Thomas Hollyman p25, Library of Congress p27; TopFoto: The British Library/HIP
p7, p9, The Granger Collection, New York p10; Wellcome Library, London: p16.

Contents

The pioneering work of Dorothy Crowfoot Hodgkin in the field of X-ray crystallography helped several of the medical scientists mentioned in this book. X-ray crystallography allowed scientists such as Francis Crick and James Watson the chance to 'see' substances in a 3D form and so helped further their study and uses in medicine. During the Second World War Hodgkin used X-ray crystallography to investigate penicillin and later used it to study vitamin B12.

What is a medical pioneer?

A medical pioneer is a person who develops new ideas or techniques in medicine, or someone who is the first to open up a new area of medicine for others to follow.

Who are medical pioneers?

Many medical pioneers are doctors, surgeons or research scientists. Some pioneers, such as Alexander Fleming, made their discovery by accident; others, such as Frederick Banting, had an idea or a theory and set out to prove it. Some medical pioneers, such as Harold Delf Gillies and Alice Hamilton, were the first people or the first representatives of their sex to establish themselves in a specific area of medicine.

The medical pioneers selected here are from all over the world. They may have developed surgical procedures, such as organ transplants, or been based in the laboratory discovering new substances that help to treat conditions such as diabetes, polio or leukaemia. Some of the pioneers have been involved in developing technology that has improved the way people are diagnosed and treated, such as magnetic resonance imaging (MRI) or the electron microscope.

The golden age of medicine

Great advances in medicine were made during the twentieth century. Technologies were invented which offered new ways of looking into the body and its cells, so helping doctors to make more reliable diagnoses. Antibiotics made surgery far safer than it had ever been and so led to further surgical advances, such as keyhole surgery and neurosurgery. Clean water and better sanitation systems greatly improved the health of the public in the nineteenth century. From the 1950s vaccines also improved people's health by protecting them from common diseases such as polio.

Overcoming challenges

The twentieth century saw two world wars, which hastened the development of some medical discoveries, and these were used to great effect. The shortage of men to fill jobs during the wars also meant that women were able to get a foothold in the medical profession – something which, until then, had been a challenge for women to overcome.

Looking to the future

Just as some of the discoveries made in the nineteenth century paved the way for breakthroughs in the twentieth century, so the twentieth century pioneers have provided valuable research and insight on which current and future pioneers can build. For example, thanks in part to the work of pioneers Crick and Watson, we are now entering a fascinating new age of genetic engineering that is likely to have very far-reaching effects on our lives.

Genetic engineering means making changes to the DNA of a living creature. Some creatures are cloned, or even engineered to develop new kinds of species. Here, a biologist holds the offspring of a genetically engineered pig.

"The Nobel Prize is fine, but the drugs I've developed are rewards in themselves." *Gertrude Elion*

Alexander Fleming

Founder of the 'Miracle Drug'

"When I woke up just after dawn on September 28, 1928, I certainly didn't plan to revolutionize all medicine by discovering the world's first antibiotic, or bacteria killer ... But I guess that was exactly what I did."

Alexander Fleming

Name Sir Alexander Fleming

Born 6 August 1881 in Lochfield, Ayrshire, Scotland

Died 11 March 1955

Studied Medicine at St Mary's Hospital, Paddington, London

Best known as The scientist who discovered penicillin, the 'miracle drug'

Honours and awards Fleming was knighted in 1944, and in 1945, together with Florey and Chain, he received the Nobel Prize.

Interesting fact Fleming was a popular figure in the London art scene and treated many famous painters and artists. He would often be repaid for his medical skills with a painted portrait of himself!

Until almost the mid-twentieth century doctors could do little to treat serious infections. They could amputate an infected limb or remove a swollen appendix, but they had to rely on the patient's own immune system to overcome any infection. In many cases patients were unable to fight the infection and they died. Doctors were powerless to act. But in 1928 Alexander Fleming's momentous discovery changed the face of medicine, making surgery and the treatment of infections more successful than ever before.

The early days

Alexander Fleming grew up on a sheep farm in a remote part of Scotland, spending a great deal of time exploring the streams and valleys near his home. As a teenager, he moved to London and worked for several years as a shipping clerk.

In 1901 he inherited £250 from his uncle, enabling 20-year-old Alexander to train as a doctor.

The amazing discovery

It was in 1928 at St Mary's Hospital that Fleming made his accidental discovery. As part of his research into influenza ('flu), Fleming 'grew' or cultivated a type of 'flu bacteria in glass petri dishes containing jelly. Though he was a brilliant scientist, Fleming was known to run a chaotic laboratory. One morning he noticed that a type of mould had destroyed the 'flu bacteria in dishes he had accidentally left uncovered for several days. Tests showed that this was a substance called Penicillium notatum – similar to the mould that grows on stale bread. Fleming called it 'penicillin'.

Unfortunately Fleming lacked the skills to convert penicillin into a pure form that could be given to patients, and his research came to a halt for 12 years. In 1941 however, an Australian scientist, Howard Florey, and a German chemist, Ernst Chain, worked out how to produce a pure form of penicillin. Mass production of the 'miracle drug' began in 1943. The timing was perfect; thousands of lives were saved during the Second World War by using penicillin to treat wounds that previously would have been fatal.

International hero

Though he was a shy character, following his Nobel Prize Fleming enjoyed a decade of fame and travel. He died an international hero, and received Britain's highest honour in death when his ashes were interred in St Paul's Cathedral, London.

This petri dish shows penicillin mould grown on an agar jelly. The mould is preventing the growth of the bacteria in the jelly (shown by the darker areas), just as it did in Fleming's original petri dishes of 1928.

Twentieth-century legacy

Fleming's discovery of penicillin changed the face of medicine by introducing antibiotics (bacteria killers). Penicillin has saved and continues to save many millions of lives. Its discovery paved the way for many other types of antibiotics to be developed, making possible the treatment of deadly diseases such as meningitis and tuberculosis.

Harold Delf Gillies

A Pioneer in Plastic Surgery

"Within us all there is an overwhelming urge to change something ugly and useless into some other thing more beautiful and more functional."

Harold Delf Gillies

The First World War of 1914-18 presented a huge challenge to the medical profession, particularly to surgeons. The destructive weapons used in the war resulted in more horrific injuries than had ever been seen before. Soldiers, particularly those who fought in the trenches, were often exposed to devastating facial injuries. A young doctor named Harold Delf Gillies realised that the war demanded a new type of surgery. He pioneered operations that involved reconstructing the face by taking tissue from the patient's neck, chest or shoulders.

Early creativity

Gillies grew up on a farm in New Zealand. He was an artistic boy and this creativity came through in the work he did later, in reshaping and recreating disfigured faces. After his medical degree Gillies trained at the famous St Bartholomew's hospital in London where it became clear than he had a talent for specialised surgery.

Wartime plastic surgery

When World War One broke out Gillies was posted to France. There he met a French-American named

Full name Harold Delf Gillies

Born 17 June 1882, Dunedin, New Zealand

Died 10 September 1960

Studied Medicine at Gonville and Caius College, Cambridge University

Best known as The doctor who pioneered plastic and reconstructive surgery

Honours and awards Gillies was knighted in June 1930 for his services to reconstructive surgery throughout the First World War.

Interesting fact Gillies excelled in most sports, particularly cricket, golf and rowing. While at university he earned his 'blue'(the highest sporting honour) for his part in the Cambridge rowing team.

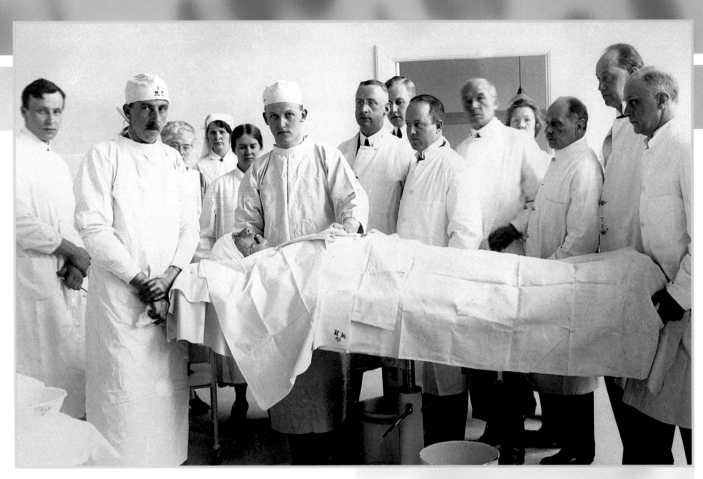

Britain's first plastic surgeon, Harold Delf Gillies, shown here with colleagues and patient, in readiness to perform pioneering plastic surgery techniques.

Valadier who specialised in jaw repair work, taking tissue from other parts of the body. Excited by Valadier's work, Gillies applied to the British Army to request that they open a plastic surgery unit. On 11 January 1916 Gillies' request was granted and he set up Britain's first plastic surgery unit at Cambridge Military Hospital in Aldershot, Surrey.

Improving lives

Rebuilding the face using tissue from other parts of the body was not a new idea, but Gillies was driven by the idea that reconstructive surgery need not be crude and 'make do'. Instead it could be creative and artistic, significantly improving life for his patients. Gillies pioneered innovative techniques (the basis of which are still used today) that involved using 'tubes' of living tissue called 'pedicle tubes' to reconstruct the face.

After the war Gillies opened a successful private clinic in London, pioneering what is known today as 'cosmetic surgery'.

Twentieth-century legacy

Gillies' work has been the forerunner to much of today's reconstructive facial and plastic or cosmetic surgery. It is carried out in cases of birth abnormalities, accident, disease or (in the case of cosmetic surgery) to improve a person's appearance. Gillies trained many doctors in his art after the war, and his principles have been adopted by plastic and reconstructive surgeons all over the world. Thanks to his expertise many people are able to lead happy, fulfilling lives.

Frederick Banting

The Diabetes Doctor

"Insulin is not a cure for diabetes;
it is a treatment."

Frederick Banting

For thousands of years the diagnosis of diabetes or 'sugar disease' meant certain death. Diabetes occurs when the body is not able to use sugars in the blood (known as glucose) due to the lack of a hormone called insulin. In 1920 a Canadian surgeon, Frederick Banting, put forward an idea to explain the cause of diabetes, and also how to treat it.

The pancreas

In the late nineteenth century scientists had made the link between diabetes and an organ in the body called the pancreas. They discovered that part of the pancreas produced a hormone called insulin. Banting realised that if he could isolate insulin from a healthy pancreas then he could use it to treat diabetic patients. He persuaded John Macleod, head of the physiology department at the University of Toronto to provide him with a laboratory, 10 diabetic dogs to use in his experiments, and an assistant.

Stabilisation of blood sugar

In May 1921 Banting and his assistant, Charles Best, began their experiments. Three months later they had their results: when insulin (extracted from the pancreas) was given to diabetic dogs, their high blood sugar levels stabilised to a normal level.

Full name Frederick Grant Banting

Born 14 November 1891 in Ontario, Canada

Died 21 February 1941

Studied Medicine at the University of Toronto

Best known as One of the scientists who discovered insulin

Honours and awards He was jointly awarded the 1923 Nobel Prize in Medicine with fellow scientist John Macleod. In 1934 Banting received a knighthood for his services to medicine.

Interesting fact Banting was a keen painter and once took part in a painting expedition above the Arctic Circle!

Banting and Best enlisted the help of a chemist to help them to purify the substance and some weeks later insulin was tried out on a 14-year-old boy who was dying of diabetes. The injection of insulin lowered his blood sugar levels and cleared him of signs of the disease.

Big breakthrough

The discovery of insulin was one of the most dramatic breakthroughs in medicine. Though it took some time to work out proper dosages and how to manufacture insulin to the correct strength and purity, it was hailed as a miracle of modern medicine. Almost overnight it seemed that diabetes had gone from being a death sentence to being a disease that could be controlled. People with the disease were given the chance to lead full and productive lives.

A wartime death

In 1938 Banting developed an interest in aviation medicine and began to work for the Royal Canadian Air Force, looking at the medical problems encountered by pilots while in the air. Ironically Banting was killed in an aeroplane crash in Newfoundland, Canada, during the Second World War, while on an official military mission.

Frederick Banting (on the right) and his assistant, Charles Best, pictured here with one of the diabetic dogs used in their research into diabetes, the 'sugar disease'.

Twentieth-century legacy

Thanks to the work of Sir Frederick Banting millions of people's lives have been saved. Modern science and technology has made high-quality insulin widely available. People who have diabetes are now able to monitor their blood sugar levels and administer insulin themselves so that they are in control of the disease and of their lives.

Jonas Salk
The Polio Philanthropist

"Who owns my polio vaccine?
The people!
Could you patent the sun?"

Jonas Salk

In 1950s America, parents lived in fear of their children being infected with the crippling disease poliomyelitis (polio), otherwise known as infantile paralysis. As many as one in every 5,000 US children were affected, and those who didn't die were confined to wheelchairs, or could only walk with the aid of leg braces or crutches.

But in 1955 a discovery made by the biologist Jonas Salk led to the eradication of a disease that had previously been affecting close to 50,000 children every year in the US alone and many millions worldwide.

The switch to medicine

Born in New York City, the son of uneducated Russian-Jewish immigrants, Salk carried the ambitions and determination of his family. Excelling at school, he graduated a year early, and went on to attend New York University, switching from law to medicine.

While director of the Virus Research Laboratory at the University of Pittsburgh School of Medicine in 1947, Salk's research into a 'flu vaccine caught the attention of the National Foundation for Infantile Paralysis (later the March of Dimes), who decided

Full name Jonas Edward Salk

Born 28 October 1914 in New York City, USA

Died 23 June 1995

Studied Medicine at New York University

Best known as The scientist who developed the polio vaccine

Honours and awards In 1977 Salk was awarded the Presidential Medal of Freedom (the highest civilian honour in the United States).

Interesting fact He established the Jonas Salk Institute for Biological Studies in La Jolla, California, with the help of architect Louis Khan, creating a building that stands as one of the masterpieces of 20th century architecture.

to fund his efforts to develop a polio vaccine. Salk's vaccine was composed of 'killed' polio virus, which retained the ability to immunise patients without running the risk of infecting them. The vaccine was given by injection and was first used in a successful trial in 1952.

Vaccine trials

On 12 April 1955, after further extensive trials, the vaccine was pronounced safe and effective. The results were remarkable, cutting the average number of US polio cases per year from over 45,000 to fewer than 1,000.

Just as remarkably perhaps, Salk never patented the vaccine, nor did he earn any money from his discovery, preferring to see it distributed as widely as possible.

Later, a Polish-American doctor named Albert Sabin developed the polio vaccine which is more widely used today, and is administered orally (by mouth). This vaccine contains a weakened form of the polio virus, which causes the body to create immunity but which does not cause the patient to suffer the illness.

During the last 40 years of his life, Jonas Salk continued with his vaccine research but also conducted research into cancer and diseases of the immune system.

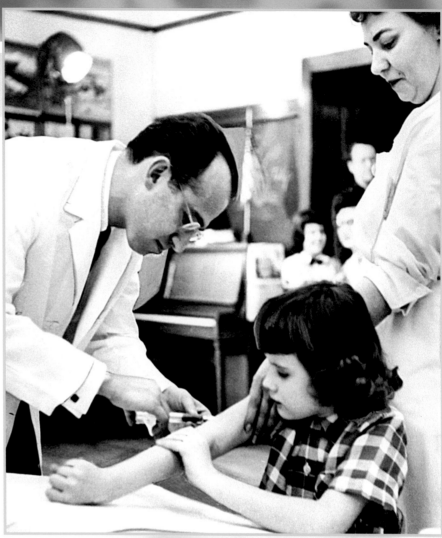

Polio is a viral infection that can cause paralysis. This picture shows Salk administering his pioneering polio vaccine to a child patient in the 1950s.

Twentieth-century legacy

Jonas Salk's discovery of a polio vaccine and his decision not to profit from his discovery, allowed for the swift distribution of the vaccine. This virtually wiped out a disease that had previously killed or crippled millions of children every year.

Nowadays virtually every child worldwide will receive polio vaccinations during their first year of life, ensuring that polio will never become established again.

Francis Crick (on the left) and James Watson

Full names Francis Harry Compton Crick; James Dewey Watson

Born (Crick) 8 June 1916 in Northamptonshire, England; (Watson) 6 April 1928 in Chicago, USA

Died (Crick) 28 July 2004

Studied Crick studied physics at University College London and Cambridge University. Watson studied zoology at the University of Chicago and University of Indiana.

Best known as The scientists who first revealed the structure of DNA

Honours and awards Crick & Watson (along with fellow scientist Maurice Wilkins) were jointly awarded the 1962 Nobel Prize for their DNA discovery.

Interesting fact During the Second World War Francis Crick worked on the design of explosive mines.

Francis Crick & James Watson

Decoders of the 'Secret of Life'

"I couldn't have got anywhere without Francis.... It could have been Crick without Watson, but certainly not Watson without Crick."

James Watson

By the 1950s scientists had a basic understanding of the role that genes played in passing on characteristics – such as skin, eye and hair colour – from one generation to another. These genes, the scientists had discovered, were contained within DNA (deoxyribonucleic acid) a kind of 'code' that determined what all living things would be like. Scientists were still puzzled, however, by the structure of DNA and how it was able to pass its 'messages' from generation to generation. Then, in 1953, two men rushed into a Cambridge pub and announced they had discovered 'the secret of life' – the structure of DNA! These men were an American biologist called James Watson and a British physicist named Francis Crick.

X-ray crystallography

The pair met in 1951 while working at the Cavendish Laboratories at Cambridge University, and together they decided to apply their minds to working out the structure of DNA.

The 1950s was an exciting time in science. A process called X-ray crystallography had been developed in the 1930s by Dorothy Hodgkin (see page 4), which scientists could use to 'photograph' complex substances such as DNA. Many scientists across the world were eager to learn the secret of DNA and among them were Crick and Watson.

The double helix

By studying the X-ray crystallography patterns developed by scientists Maurice Wilkins and Rosalind Franklin at King's College in London, Crick and Watson set about building three-dimensional models of DNA using a system of small balls and sticks. After several unsuccessful attempts, and with other scientists getting ever closer to solving the mystery, Crick and Watson finally revealed a DNA model that was arranged in a double spiral (called a helix), rather like a ladder that has been twisted.

Crick and Watson's discovery was one of the most important breakthroughs of the 20th century, since knowledge of its structure finally revealed how DNA copied itself and therefore passed on its messages to the next generation. In recognition of their work Watson and Crick were awarded the Nobel Prize in 1962, along with Wilkins. Franklin had died in 1958 and so did not receive the Nobel honour, since it can only be awarded to living recipients.

Francis Crick (on the right) and James Watson, pictured with their model of the structure of a DNA molecule, in the Medical Research Council Unit at Cambridge University.

Twentieth-century legacy

The significance of Francis Crick and James Watson's discovery today is enormous. Understanding DNA has enabled scientists to work out how genetic messages are passed between generations. Armed with this knowledge, scientists are now able to fight inherited diseases, such as heart problems or cystic fibrosis, that can be passed on from parent to child.

Gertrude Elion

Pioneering Drug Developer

"The Nobel Prize is fine, but the drugs I've developed are rewards in themselves."

Gertrude Elion

Full name Gertrude Belle Elion

Born 23 January 1918 in New York City, USA

Died 22 February 1999

Studied Chemistry at Hunter College, New York and New York University

Best known as The scientist who developed many groundbreaking drugs to treat a range of diseases and conditions.

Honours and awards In 1988 she was jointly awarded the Nobel Prize in Medicine. In 1991 she was presented with the National Medal of Science by President George Bush, who said that her work had 'transformed the world'.

Interesting fact Gertrude Elion was an avid traveller and photographer, and loved opera, ballet and the theatre.

The 1950s saw the discovery of many exciting new drug treatments. Many of these were important in advancing medical and surgical treatments. One important discovery was of immuno-suppressant drugs which would allow the body's own immune system to 'accept' donor organs – therefore leading to successful organ transplants of all types. The medical pioneer behind this and many other groundbreaking treatments during the second half of the twentieth century was Gertrude Elion.

Her childhood

Gertrude's early years were spent living above her father's dental surgery in Manhattan, New York. She had a happy childhood, enjoyed school and had a strong desire to learn. At the end of high school she could not choose what subject to study at college but, as her beloved grandfather had died of cancer when she was 15, she decided to pursue a career in chemistry in the hope of finding a cure for this terrible disease.

In the early years after college Gertrude found it difficult to find work as a chemist. There were few women working in this area and many laboratories refused to employ women altogether. She gained some experience by working in temporary jobs and studied for a master's degree at New York University at the same time. She was the only female in her chemistry class.

Her first success

When the United States entered the Second World War in 1944 it led to a shortage of male workers in civilian professions. This gave Gertrude Elion the opportunity she needed. Gertrude was hired by a laboratory called Burroughs Wellcome. She embarked on a study of disease cells and how they were made up. Within a few years her research led her to the discovery of the first successful treatments for leukaemia. She began to head large research teams and founded treatments for gout, arthritis, malaria and anti-viral treatments.

New diseases

Few scientists have matched the wide array of drugs that Gertrude Elion developed. She retired in 1983 but continued working with her old company (now called Glaxo Wellcome), helping to develop AZT, the first drug used against the AIDS virus.

She was jointly awarded the Nobel Prize in Medicine in 1988 but maintained that her aim had always been to make people well, saying that "the satisfaction of that is much greater than any prize you can get". Elion was devoted to her work throughout her life, but in later years became an avid photographer and traveller. She also developed a major interest in music, opera and ballet. Gertrude Elion died in 1999 at the age of 81.

Gertrude Elion, back in the laboratory after her Nobel Prize award. It is thanks to her patient determination that thousands of people throughout the world are able to lead healthy lives.

Twentieth-century legacy

Gertrude Elion broke down barriers for women in the male-dominated world of medical research. In addition to her groundbreaking treatment for leukaemia, she also developed drugs to treat arthritis, malaria and other bacterial infections. All of these treatments have helped millions of people all over the world. Her work has set a standard in pharmaceutical research, and in years to come, thanks to her methods, scientists will be better equipped to find the cures for the world's major diseases, including cancer – the disease that Elion had always wanted to wipe out.

Christiaan Barnard

The 'Film Star' Surgeon

"I was happy when I saw the heart beating again. We did not stand up or cheer or anything like that. I didn't even inform the hospital authorities that I was going to do the operation."

Christiaan Barnard

Full name Christiaan Neethling Barnard

Born 8 November 1922 in Beaufort West, South Africa

Died 2 September 2001

Studied Medicine at the University of Cape Town, South Africa, and cardiothoracic (heart and lung) surgery at the University of Minnesota, USA

Best known as The surgeon who carried out the first successful human heart transplant

Honours and awards In 1972 he was made Professor of Surgical Science at the University of Cape Town, South Africa. In 1984 on his retirement from surgery he was awarded the title of Professor Emeritus.

Interesting fact After his first successful heart transplant, Barnard became known as the 'film star surgeon'. He appeared on the covers of magazines, toured the world and kept the company of famous and glamorous film stars such as Sophia Loren. He visited the US President and the Pope, both of whom congratulated him on his work.

The mid-twentieth century was an exciting time in medical surgery. Many groundbreaking organ transplants had been performed, but no-one had yet carried out a successful human heart transplant. On 3 December 1967 a South African heart surgeon by the name of Christiaan Barnard led a 30-strong team in a nine-hour operation to change this, making medical history and becoming one of the most celebrated medical pioneers of the century.

A careeer in medicine

The son of a church pastor, Christiaan Barnard and his four brothers grew up in humble surroundings. One of his brothers died from heart disease at the age of five, which is thought to have influenced Christiaan's choice of career. As a young man he walked five miles each day to study medicine at Cape Town University. For several years he worked as a family doctor on the Western Cape.

Pioneering surgery

In the late 1950s Christiaan Barnard went to America to study cardiothoracic surgery. By the 1960s he had returned to Cape Town and made his name as an excellent heart and lung surgeon at the Groote Schuur Hospital. One of his patients, a 54-year-old man named Louis Washkansky, suffering from diabetes and incurable heart disease, chose to undergo pioneering heart surgery though he knew his chances of survival were slim.

The heart of a young traffic accident victim was transplanted into Washkansky's body and medical history was made. Though Washkansky died 18 days later of a lung infection, Barnard had pioneered many important medical advances and overnight he became an international hero. The handsome and photogenic young surgeon received a great deal of media attention and became a well-known figure.

Later work

Barnard continued to be passionate about his work. He pioneered further heart operations such as designing artificial valves for the heart, and using monkeys' hearts to keep very ill people alive.

He did not stop performing surgery until 1983 when arthritis in his hands prevented him from continuing. Instead he took up writing and went to live on a 32,000-acre sheep farm and game preserve in the region of South Africa where he grew up. Christiaan Barnard died in 2001 while on holiday in Cyprus.

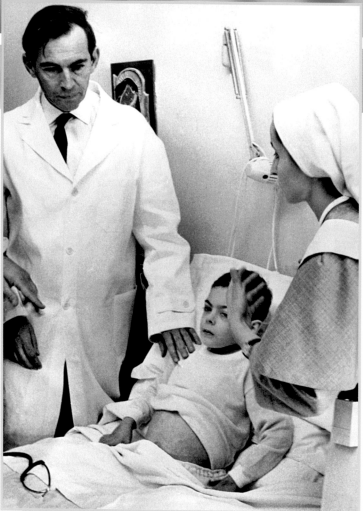

Christiaan Barnard carried out many operations on children with heart problems. He said he would like to be remembered more for these operations than for the heart transplants he performed, saying how satisfying it was to give a child the chance to live a normal life.

Twentieth-century legacy

Christiaan Barnard's work was a milestone in the development of life-extending surgery. Thanks to his pioneering techniques, heart transplantation is now such a well-refined procedure that around 90 per cent of patients who undergo a heart transplant today can expect to survive for at least five years.

Benjamin Carson

Eminent Brain Surgeon

"I said to myself, 'What's an area where you could become an authority very quickly?' and I said, 'The brain, because nobody knows anything about the brain.'"

Benjamin Carson

Neuroscience (the science of the brain and nervous system) took many forms before the 20th century, but often relied upon the notion of 'spirits' and other pseudo (false) scientific ideas. The 20th century saw enormous advances in the field of neurosurgery, aided by other medical advances such as MRI (see page 29) and keyhole surgery. In 1987 a pioneering neurosurgeon made medical history with a groundbreaking operation to separate a pair of conjoined twins. That surgeon was Dr Benjamin Carson and his story is so inspiring that a movie has been made about his life!

'Class dummy'

When Ben Carson was eight his parents divorced, leaving his mother Sonya to raise Ben and his brother. Uneducated and living in poverty, Sonya Carson took cleaning jobs to make ends meet. Ben Carson was known as the 'class dummy' at school; bullied by other children and ignored by his teachers. His mother decided to turn things around for her sons; she banned television and insisted that her boys read two library books a week.

Full name Benjamin Solomon Carson

Born 18 September 1951 in Detriot, Michigan, USA

Studied Psychology at Yale University and medicine at the University of Michigan

Best known as The first neurosurgeon to separate a pair of conjoined twins successfully.

Honours and awards In 2008 President George W Bush presented Dr Carson with the Presidential Medal of Freedom. This is the United States' highest civilian honour and was awarded for his work as a surgeon and for his efforts to improve the lives of many children in the USA.

Interesting fact Benjamin Carson made an appearance as himself in the movie *Stuck on You* (2003), starring Matt Damon and Greg Kinnear. In the film he appears as a surgeon who is to separate the conjoined twins.

Ben's reading gave him a hunger for knowledge and his schoolwork improved. After graduating with honours from high school, he attended Yale University where he studied for a degree in psychology. After Yale he went to medical school and began to study neurosurgery. A brilliant surgeon, he became the Director of Paediatric Neurosurgery at the world-famous Johns Hopkins Hospital in Baltimore at the age of 32.

Successful separation

The Binder twins were born joined at the back of the head. In the past, operations to separate twins who were joined in this way had always failed, resulting in the death of one, or both, of the children. Carson agreed to perform the operation and after 22 hours, supported by a team of 70, the twins were successfully separated and are now able to survive independent of each other.

Further successful twin operations followed in 1997 and 2003 as well as other pioneering brain surgery procedures. Today Ben Carson is in demand as a public speaker. He spends much of his time motivating young people, and is one of the co-founders of the Carson Scholars' Fund, which acknowledges young people of all backgrounds for their exceptional achievements. He has also authored several best-selling books: *Gifted Hands, The Ben Carson Story* (released as a movie in 2009 starring Cuba Gooding Jr as Ben Carson), *The Big Picture* and *Think Big*.

In 1987 Benjamin Carson made medical history with a groundbreaking operation to separate the Binder twins, who were joined at the back of the head.

Twentieth-century legacy

New techniques in neurosurgery are on-going, but Benjamin Carson's work has pushed forward the boundaries in complex paediatric neurosurgery such as the separation of twins joined at the head or by performing a hemispherectomy (removing one half of the brain) to control seizures (fits) in infants.

Eleanor Davies-Colley

First Woman in the Operating Theatre

"She was a dedicated surgeon who was adored by her patients."

J Fowler of the Royal College of Surgeons, in 2004, describing Eleanor Davies-Colley

The eighteenth century saw an explosion of interest in surgery, both among the general public and by students considering it as a career. Throughout the eighteenth and nineteenth centuries men took up surgical posts, but women were excluded as it was thought to be an unsuitable job for a woman.

At the turn of the twentieth century things started to change; some women were qualifying from medical schools but still faced disapproval from male colleagues. However, the First World War of 1914-18 led to a shortage of doctors that women were able to fill. One of these pioneering female surgeons was Eleanor Davies-Colley.

School days

Eleanor attended Baker Street High School and Queen's College, both in London. On leaving school she worked with poor children in London's East End before studying for her medical degree.

Her first medical post was as house surgeon at the New Hospital for Women (now called the Elizabeth

---

Full name Eleanor Davies-Colley

Born 21 August 1874 in Petworth, Sussex, UK

Died 10 December 1934

Studied Medicine at the London School of Medicine for Women and University of London

Best known as One of the first women in the UK to become a surgeon

Honours and awards In 1911 Davies-Colley became the first female fellow of the Royal College of Surgeons.

Interesting fact Her family had over 200 years of medical tradition. Her father was a surgeon and her grandfather was a hospital treasurer, both at Guy's Hospital in London.

Garrett Anderson Hospital) in London. In 1911, along with her colleague and medical trainer Maud Chadburn, she began to raise funds to open a hospital for women.

Role of women's hospitals

At that time women's hospitals served a double purpose; they existed to improve the medical care for women but also provided a career for many female doctors and surgeons, since many hospitals refused to employ women.

By 1916, helped by her cousin, feminist and publisher Harriet Shaw Weaver, and other feminists, enough money had been raised to open the South London Hospital for Women and Children. The 80-bed, purpose-built hospital, staffed entirely by women was opened on Clapham Common in London by Queen Mary on 4 July.

In 1917 Eleanor Davies-Colley became one of the founding members of the Medical Women's Federation. This organisation was concerned with helping to advance the careers of women in the medical profession.

In memory

Eleanor Davies-Colley's career as a surgeon spanned almost 30 years. In 2004 the Royal College of Surgeons' lecture theatre was refurbished and dedicated to the memory of Eleanor and her lasting contribution as a pioneering woman surgeon.

The South London Hospital for Women and Children. Eleanor Davies-Colley worked here from its opening in 1916 until her death, holding several positions including senior surgeon.

Twentieth-century legacy

Eleanor Davies-Colley established her career in the male-dominated field of surgery. From 1948 all medical schools finally admitted women and since then there has been a steady increase in intake. Today women are in the majority in our medical schools. Though only six per cent of surgeons in the UK are female, this figure is rising and it is thanks to the hard work and excellence of Eleanor Davies-Colley and other pioneers like her that women now have the free choice to enter the surgical profession.

Karl Landsteiner
The Man with Blood on his Mind

Until the early 1900s scientists believed that everybody's blood was the same. Giving a blood transfusion was dangerous; sometimes it was successful, but often it was not.

When transfusions did not work this was because the blood from the donor 'clumped together' in the recipient and usually killed them. Karl Landsteiner, an Austrian scientist, reasoned that there must be differences in the make-up of blood from one person to the next.

The four blood groups
In 1901, after an exhausting year of testing many blood samples, Landsteiner concluded that there were three main human blood groups – A, B and C (later renamed O). Two of Landsteiner's colleagues identified a fourth blood type, AB, a year later.

A focus on research
Karl Landsteiner was a brilliant student who was accepted to study medicine at the age of 17. He saw that the future of medicine lay in research and so opted to become a research scientist rather than a doctor.

Landsteiner's legacy
The discovery of blood types saved lives in hospitals and on the battlefields of the First World War where transfusions took place on a large scale. Later on, blood types would also be used to help the police solve crimes by testing blood samples found at a crime scene.

Full name Karl Landsteiner
Born 14 June 1868 in Vienna, Austria
Died 26 June 1943
Studied Medicine at the University of Vienna
Best known as The first scientist to discover different blood types and to classify blood into groups
Honours and awards Landsteiner was awarded the Nobel Prize in 1930 for his identification of blood types.
Interesting fact Though he was an eminent scientist, Karl Landsteiner was a private man who disliked publicity. He rarely gave interviews to reporters and seldom gave speeches, even though he was constantly invited to so.

Ernst Ruska

Inventor of the Electron Microscope

At the start of the twentieth century microscopic science had almost reached a standstill. Scientists wanted to study the minute structures of particles but microscopes at that time relied on light. This meant that even the most powerful light microscope did not have the magnification to view the things that scientists needed to see in order to push their research forward.

Electron particles

Ernst Ruska, a student at the University of Berlin, wondered if a microscope could be invented that acted like a normal light microscope but used a beam of particles called electrons, rather than light, to view things.

Huge magnification

In 1932 Ruska and his partner, a German scientist called Max Knoll, invented the first electron microscope. Though it was a very basic model and was not yet capable of being used in laboratories, the microscope was still capable of magnifying objects 400 times. Modern-day electron microscopes can now magnify an object 2 million times, but they are still based on Ruska's original model.

Electron microscopes are vital to laboratories all over the world and, thanks to Ruska, many significant advances have been made, not only in medicine, but also in genetics, chemistry and engineering.

Full name Ernst August Friedrich Ruska

Born 25 December 1906 in Heidelberg, Germany

Died 27 May 1988

Studied Engineering at the Technical Universities of Munich and Berlin

Best known as The scientist who invented the electron microscope

Honours and awards He was jointly awarded the Nobel Prize in Physics in 1986. The Nobel Society described the electron microscope as 'one of the most important inventions of the 20th century'.

Interesting fact As a child Ruska was fascinated with microscopes and telescopes, and in particular with the microscope that his father kept in his study. Ernst and his seven siblings were strictly forbidden to touch the microscope, which fired Ernst's interest even more!

Virginia Apgar

Pioneer in Babies' Health

The 1950s saw great breakthroughs in obstetrics, the branch of medicine concerned with childbirth, and it is thanks to Virginia Apgar that the health of newborn babies from this time was significantly improved. The Apgar Test that she developed continues to affect every newborn baby today as it is the standard for evaluating a newborn's health all over the world.

Achievement

Virginia Apgar was determined to be a doctor. In 1937, though few women at that time even attended college, and in spite of financial hardship, she achieved her goal. Her study of anaesthesia during childbirth and the effects that it had on the newborn baby led her to develop the Apgar Test. The test, given one and five minutes after birth, monitors the breathing, heart rate, muscle tone, reflex response and colour of a newborn baby. It enables doctors to assess whether further medical treatment is necessary for the survival or general health of the baby.

Public health

In 1959 Apgar earned a master's degree in public health and became increasingly interested in the health of children in a broader way. She devoted herself to the study of birth defects, and how the public can be educated to prevent them, such as by ensuring that folic acid is present in the diet of pregnant women. She became a director at the National Foundation for Infantile Paralysis.

Full name Virginia Apgar

Born 7 June 1909 in Westfield, New Jersey, USA

Died 7 August 1974

Studied Zoology at Mount Holyoke College, New York, followed by medicine at Columbia University Medical School

Best known as The woman who pioneered the 'Apgar Test', to evaluate the health of newborn babies

Honours and awards In 1949 Dr Apgar was the first woman to be made a professor, and in 1973 the first woman to receive the Gold Medal for Distinguished Achievement in Medicine, both awarded by the College of Surgeons and Physicians at Columbia University. In 1994 she was pictured on a US postage stamp as part of the 'Great Americans' series.

Interesting fact A dedicated musician since childhood Virginia Apgar loved to play the cello and violin in her spare time, but in the 1950s she began to build her own stringed instruments. Her apartment was filled with woodworking tools and a workbench!

Alice Hamilton

Pioneer of Health at Work

Since the Industrial Revolution of the late 19th century, people had started to become aware of dangers in the workplace and the illnesses that were caused by working in certain jobs. In 1907 a medically trained woman called Alice Hamilton who had developed a special interest in 'industrial medicine', noted that little research was being done on this in America – so set out to make changes.

Unhealthy working conditions

In 1897 Alice Hamilton was appointed professor of pathology at the Women's Medical School of Northwestern University in Chicago. While in Chicago Alice noted how the health problems of the poorer residents were caused by unsafe conditions and exposure to toxic chemicals, including lead dust, which occurred in the course of their jobs. Employers meanwhile were firing these sick workers.

Change for the good

In 1910 Hamilton was appointed to the new Occupational Diseases Commission of Illinois, the first investigative body in the United States. She focused on dangers present at work including poisons, toxic gases and dust. Her findings were significant initially in America, but as the field of occupational health became established and spread to other countries, the health and working conditions of people all over the world improved significantly.

Full name Alice Hamilton

Born 27 February 1869 in Fort Wayne, Indiana, USA

Died 22 September 1970

Studied Medicine at University of Michigan, USA

Best known as A leading pioneer in the field of occupational (work) health

Honours and awards She was the first woman professor at the world famous Harvard Medical School and the first woman to receive the Lasker Award in public health in 1947.

Interesting fact Alice Hamilton lived until she was 100 years old.

Robert A Good

Founder of Modern Immunology

A paediatrician and pathologist, Dr Robert Good earned himself a reputation worldwide over 30 years for his research at the University of Minnesota. He began his work on immunity in the 1940s helping to identify the cells in the body that work together to fight off infections. In 1965 he drew attention to his work when he presented evidence that the tonsils (thought to be useless in the body) were actually important to the immune defence system and therefore should only be removed in serious cases.

The breakthrough operation

In 1968 Good led the team that carried out the first bone marrow transplant. Bone marrow contains many cells that make up the body's defence system, so healthy bone marrow is transferred into a person with a diseased immune system. The pioneering transplant was made on a four-month-old boy with a severe immune deficiency; the boy made a remarkable recovery and grew up to be a healthy adult.

Cancer treatments

Robert A Good held many distinguished positions but in 1972 he was made president of the Sloan-Kettering Institute for Cancer Research. This role enabled him to continue his research into the body's defences, especially in regard to cancer. At the All Children's Hospital in Florida, where he served from 1985, he developed a bone marrow transplantation programme for treating leukaemia as well as studying the influence of food and nutrition on the diseases of old age.

Full name Robert Alan Good

Born 21 May 1922 in Crosby, Minnesota, USA

Died 13 June 2003

Studied Medicine at the University of Minnesota

Best known as The surgeon who performed the first successful bone marrow transplant

Honours and awards He was awarded the Albert Lasker Medical Research Award in 1970 to recognise his work in immunology and in helping to combat fatal diseases.

Interesting fact As a student Good developed a polio-like illness that left him partially paralysed. He eventually recovered from the illness but walked with a limp for the rest of his life.

Paul Lauterbur
Developer of MRI

The development of X-rays in 1895 ushered in an era of technological medicine. X-rays were used to diagnose problems in the body, but after the Second World War their use was regulated, so other imaging techniques – or ways of looking into the body – started to be developed. Paul Lauterbur developed the idea of magnetic resonance imaging (MRI) – producing images of a patient's body with the use of radio waves, doing away with exploratory surgery to diagnose illnesses and conditions.

Idyllic childhood

After an idyllic childhood, surrounded by pets and living on his parents' farm, Lauterbur was drafted into the US army. It was during this time that he began to investigate the structure of materials and molecules. From this the seeds of an idea about MRI started to grow.

Non-invasive alternative

Back in the laboratory, Lauterbur found exploratory work done on cancer-bearing rats distasteful, and so began to develop the idea of a non-invasive alternative to surgery. He developed MRI and thanks to further development of his idea by fellow scientist Peter Mansfield, MRI scanners were introduced into hospitals in the 1980s. There are now more than 22,000 MRI scanners around the world and 60 million MRI examinations are carried out every year. MRI is diagnosing a wide range of illnesses and saving millions of lives.

Paul Lauterbur is seen here (on the right) with Sir Peter Mansfield.

Full name Paul Christian Lauterbur

Born 6 May 1929 in Sidney, Ohio, USA

Died 27 March 2007

Studied Chemistry at the Case Western Reserve University and the University of Pittsburgh

Best known as The chemist who developed magnetic resonance imaging (MRI)

Honours and awards Lauterbur was jointly awarded the 2003 Nobel Prize for Physiology or Medicine with Sir Peter Mansfield, for his work on MRI.

Interesting fact As a teenager Paul Lauterbur enjoyed conducting science experiments so much that he built his own laboratory in the basement of his parents' house.

Timeline

1901 Karl Landsteiner first identifies human blood groupings.

1903 Marie Curie is the first woman to win the Nobel Prize for her work on radioactivity.

1908 Suffragettes chain themselves to the railings of 10 Downing Street to protest about women's right to vote.

1910 Alice Hamilton is appointed to the first Occupational Diseases Commission in the United States.

1911 Eleanor Davies-Colley becomes the first female fellow of the Royal College of Surgeons.

1914-18 The First World War

1916 Harold Delf Gillies opens the UK's first plastic surgery unit.

1920 Frederick Banting discovers the cause of diabetes and how to treat it; women in the USA are given the right to vote.

1928 Alexander Fleming discovers penicillin; in the UK women over the age of 21 are given the vote.

1932 Ernst Ruska invents the first electron microscope.

1934 Dorothy Hodgkin uses X-ray crystallography to obtain 'photographs' of the structure of insulin.

1939-45 The Second World War

1948 The National Health Service is introduced in the UK, giving everyone free access to health care.

1949 Virginia Apgar develops the Apgar Test to assess the health of newborn babies.

1953 Crick and Watson discover the structure of DNA.

1955 Jonas Salk develops a vaccine for polio.

1962 Rachel Carson publishes her famous book 'Silent Spring', alerting the world to the dangers of pollution from chemicals and radiation.

1967 Christiaan Barnard performs the first successful human heart transplant.

1968 Robert A Good carries out the first successful bone marrow transplant.

1969 The first steps are taken on the Moon.

1978 The world's first 'test tube baby' is born.

1986 The Chernobyl disaster: a nuclear power plant in the Soviet Union (now Ukraine) explodes, spreading radioactive material across Europe, killing 47 people, and causing a wide range of radiation-related cancers in adults, children and unborn babies.

1987 Benjamin Carson performs the first successful operation to separate conjoined twins.

1989 The Berlin Wall comes down, reunifying East and West Germany.

1990 The Gulf War begins.

1991 The Human Genome Project begins. It is used to identify the 20,000-25,000 genes in human DNA. The 'mapping' of human genes is an important step in the development of medicines and health care.

1996 'Dolly the Sheep' is cloned – the first mammal to be cloned from the cells of an adult sheep.

Glossary

administer To give out or to supply a medical drug to cure an illness or a condition.

amputate To cut off a limb during a surgical operation.

anaesthesia Drugs, usually given to a patient during medical procedures or during surgery, that result in partial or total loss of sensation, to stop the patient feeling pain.

antibiotics Medicines, such as penicillin, which destroy or slow down the growth of bacteria.

antibodies Proteins made by the body to protect itself from 'foreign' substances such as bacteria or viruses.

blood transfusion A medical procedure in which blood is transferred from one person (the donor) to another (the recipient). This is usually done in cases where a patient has lost a lot of blood, for example in an accident or during complex surgery.

cardiothoracic The medical term to refer to the heart and lungs.

cloned An animal or plant that is produced from the cells of another, and therefore is genetically identical.

conjoined twins Identical twins who did not separate completely before birth. Conjoined twins are physically joined together and often share some organs.

diabetes A medical condition in which a lack of the hormone insulin means that sugars are not absorbed properly in the body.

DNA – deoxyribonucleic acid A substance that carries genetic information and is found in the cells of almost all creatures.

electron microscope A microscope that uses electrons rather than visible light to produce magnified images.

feminist A person who supports equal rights for women.

genetics The branch of science that deals with heredity, and how characteristics in human beings are passed from generation to generation.

hormone A substance produced by living things that is used to stimulate cells or tissues.

immune system The system of antibodies in the blood that defends the body against bacteria, viruses and other harmful substances.

immunology The branch of medicine concerned with the structure and function of the immune system.

immuno-suppressant A type of drug that is used to stop the production of antibodies. Immuno-suppressants are often used in organ transplantation to prevent recipient's body 'rejecting' an organ transplanted from a donor.

Industrial Revolution A period of great change in the late 18th century. New industries developed rapidly, new inventions were discovered and the way in which things were produced changed. Work became based in factories rather than in homes.

keyhole surgery A type of non-invasive surgery that relies on making a small cut in the body and performing surgery through this opening.

magnetic resonance imaging A test that takes pictures of the soft tissues of the body. The pictures are clearer than X-rays.

neurosurgery Surgery performed on the nervous system, including brain surgery.

non-invasive Surgery that does not involve the use of instruments and other objects into the body. An example of non-invasive surgery is keyhole surgery.

obstetrics The branch of medicine that is concerned with childbirth.

organ transplants A procedure in which an organ is moved from a donor's body to a recipient's body to replace a damaged or failing organ with a working one.

paediatric The branch of medicine concerned with children and the diseases and conditions that can affect them.

patented When an invention or discovery is patented it means that the inventor has the right to make, use or sell that invention.

pathologist A medical person who studies the causes and effects of disease.

pharmaceutical A term that refers to medicines.

philanthropist A person who helps others either by good deeds or donating money.

seizures A type of fit brought about due to a chemical imbalance in the body.

vaccine A substance injected into the body which produces antibodies that can fight a specific disease.

Index

20th Century Lives

Contents of titles in the series:

Adventurers

978 0 7502 5820 3

1. What is an adventurer?
2. Robert Scott
3 Amelia Earhart
4. Francis Chichester
5. Jacques Cousteau
6. Thor Heyerdahl
7. Edmund Hillary & Tenzing Norgay
8. Neil Armstrong
9. Ranulf Fiennes
10. Yuri Gagarin & Valentina Tereshkova
11. Matthew Henson
12. Ernest Shackleton
13. Amy Johnson
14. Antoine de Saint-Exupéry
15 Miles Hilton-Barber
16. Benedict Allen

Campaigners

978 0 7502 5822 7

1   What is a campaigner?
2   Mohandas K Gandhi
3   Helen Keller
4   Rachel Carson
5   Abbé Pierre
6   Nelson Mandela
7   Peter Benenson
8   Martin Luther King
9   Chico Mendes
10 Aung San Suu Kyi
11 Emmeline Pankhurst
12 Bertrand Russell
13 Azucenza Villaflor
14 Wangari Maathai
15 Bob Geldof
16 Arundhati Roy

Medical Pioneers

978 0 7502 5823 4

1   What is a medical pioneer?
2   Alexander Fleming
3   Harold Delf Gillies
4   Frederick Banting
5   Jonas Salk
6   Francis Crick and James Watson
7   Gertrude Elion
8   Christiaan Barnard
9   Benjamin Carson
10 Eleanor Davies-Colley
11 Karl Landsteiner
12 Ernst Ruska
13 Virginia Apgar
14 Alice Hamilton
15 Robert A Good
16 Paul Lauterbur

Sporting Heroes

978 0 7502 5821 0

1   What makes a sporting hero?
2   Babe Ruth
3   Donald Bradman
4   Jesse Owens
5   Pelé
6   Muhammad Ali
7   Steffi Graf
8   Ayrton Senna
9   Tanni Grey-Thompson
10 Jonah Lomu
11 Jack Nicklaus
12 Eddy Merckx
13 Mark Spitz
14 Yasuhiro Yamashita
15 Jayne Torvill and Christopher Dean
16 Michael Jordan

WAYLAND